Felines Opine

God from a Feline Point of View

Anita Aurit

Felines Opine – God from a feline point of view

FORWARD

Who is The Tribe of Five and why are they opining?

The Tribe of Five is a group of very opinionated felines who have thoughts on many things. They share their thoughts regularly on their blog, Feline Opines.net. God is an important part of our lives and, as The Tribe has opinions on everything, they decided humans should be able to read their thoughts on such an important subject.

I hope this little book will provide you with smiles and a new purrrspective on these Scriptures.

Purrs & Head Bonks,
Anita Aurit
Purrsonal Assistant and General Lackey to The Tribe of Five

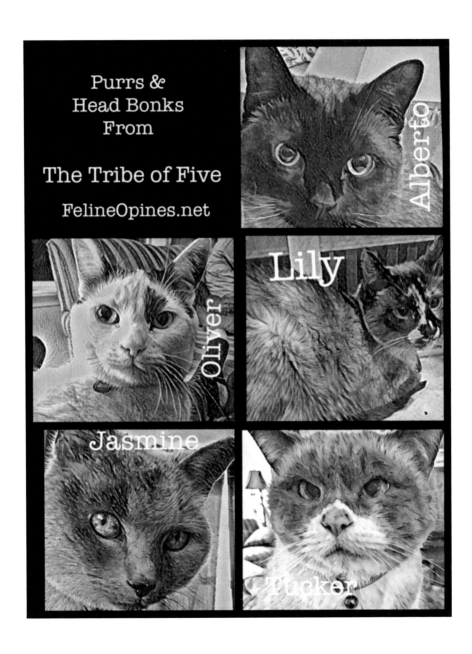

GOD'S CREATION OF ANIMALS

Genesis 1:24-27 NLT
"Then God said, "Let the earth produce every sort of animal, each producing offspring of the same kind—livestock, small animals that scurry along the ground, and wild animals." And that is what happened. God made all sorts of wild animals, livestock, and small animals, each able to produce offspring of the same kind. And God saw that it was good."

Alberto Opines
I am a lean, mean stalking machine. I quite enjoy watching the antics of the furry, scurrying animals I see outside. It's a good thing I can see what goes on out there or I'd think the only animals God created were cats! The Female Human says she feels closer to God when she interacts with His creation (well, most of His creation; she does not like snakes). She says, "The beauty of God's creation is a sign of God's great love for us." I am assuming she is including The Tribe of Five in the "us" part.

When I think of how complex God's creation is, it boggles this feline mind. God made so many animals, most I've never seen. He designed them so they all could have little versions of themselves. The "same kind" part of this verse makes me a bit skeptical. I am a sleek, handsome blue-eyed Siamese (at least I look like a Siamese). My brother is a rather rotund black and white feline with green eyes and a black heart above his eye. No one could say we look like "the same kind".

God likes animals. It's in the Bible. This verse says that after God created the animals, He looked at His work and said it was good. That means that God looks at this little cat and thinks I'm good too. I wish humans would understand this applies to them as well. Sometimes I get the impression you humans don't appreciate how God made you. If God says His creation is good, then I believe it, I mean, he created me didn't He?

GOD MAKES THE HUMANS RESPONSIBLE FOR ANIMALS
Psalm 8: 6-8 NLT

"You gave them charge of everything You made, putting all things under their authority—the flocks and the herds and all the wild animals, the birds in the sky, the fish in the sea, and everything that swims the ocean currents."

Tucker Opines

As the Alpha of the Tribe of Five (and of course, the feline in charge) I've seen a lot in my fourteen years. It is good that God expects you humans to take care of everything. Without opposable thumbs it would be very difficult for us to open our cans of food or clean our litter boxes. And, as I am portly, cross-eyed and a bit lazy, I do not find menial labor attractive.

This verse says the humans are in charge of the flocks and the herds. There are two issues here. I'm not sure if you'd call five felines a flock or a herd. We prefer the word "tribe". Whatever He calls us, I'm grateful that my humans take this verse to heart and look after us well. The second issue I have is I with the part of the verse that says God put the humans in charge of everything. Anyone who lives with a cat knows very well that no one is in charge of a feline. I prefer to use the word "assistant" when it comes to humans obeying God's edict to care for His creation. Still, I must admit that this tribe is thankful that our Humans believe in obeying God's commands. They take wonderful care of us. I hope that all you humans take good care of the animals God has given you.

ANIMALS AND THEIR NAMES

Genesis 2:19 NLT

"*So the LORD God formed from the ground all the wild animals and all the birds of the sky. He brought them to the man to see what he would call them, and the man chose a name for each one.*"

Oliver Opines

I may not be as wise as our Alpha, Tucker, but this stout little feline finds it pretty amazing that God brought every animal to Adam to have him name them. Every animal! That must have taken a long time! And Adam did a very good job, if I do say so myself. He didn't take any shortcuts, he named them ALL. If I were Adam, I'd have probably just lumped the crocodile and alligator together and called the deer, elk and antelope by one name. Adam was very conscientious about obeying God. Our Human says this is just another way that God shows how He cares for His creation. Animals were important enough to each have their own name. God does not take His creation lightly.

I must say though, sometimes the humans are a bit off on the naming thing. For instance, who names their cat after a famous cyclist? Our humans do and so my brother came to be known as Alberto Contador. I guess it's because Al is a lean mean moving machine. And they named me Oliver, after Oliver Twist. This is because when we came to live with them I was the runt of the litter. I was tiny, fragile and always hungry. Today I am a portly little fellow with a very round face and full cheeks, and a great fondness for food. Whether we resemble our names today or not, having special names all our own and selected by the Male and Female human is wonderful. I hope all you humans are thoughtful about the names you give your fur kids, keeping the tradition God started with Adam.

CARING FOR ANIMALS

Proverbs 12:10 NLT

"The godly care for their animals, but the wicked are always cruel."

Lily Opines

I will never understand why people don't take care of animals. God made us (so different and so beautiful) but still humans will ignore us or dump us off when we're too much trouble. I'm thankful that the Female Human saw me at the shelter and decided I needed to come home with her. I am sure it was my funny little blotchy face and my round eyes that captivated her. The Female Human says that godly wisdom should affect all of life, even the way people treat God's creation, especially their animals. She believes that how humans treat their animals has a bearing on how they treat other humans.

The Male Human makes fun of my big round eyes and my rather unusual coloring but he pets me, loves me and cares for me. There's always a spot for me on his lap. The Male and Female human take godly care of us and are never cruel. Do you take godly care of the critters in your home?

GOD VALUES ALL OF HIS CREATION

Luke 12:6 (NLT)

"What is the price of five sparrows—two copper coins? Yet God does not forget a single one of them. "

Jasmine Opines

Evidently there are humans who believe that some animals are more   important than others. When my brother Tucker and I were rescued, many humans wanted to adopt us because we looked like fancy, expensive kitties. I must admit, I am a beautiful little diva with deep blue eyes, tiny paws and lovely coloring. But neither Tucker nor I are fancy kitties. Our feline family was quite a diverse litter and regardless of our appearance, we are all mutts. I doubt any humans would have paid two copper coins for any of our siblings.

I watch the little birds at upstairs feeder. If God cares for the sparrows and the tiny chickadees then of course He must care for rescued kitties (even those who are not pure bred). And if God cares for sparrows and kitties and other animals, think how much He loves you humans!

God's eyes are on the sparrow, the humans and the kitties too, fancy or not. We may not all be "pure breeds" but everything God created is precious to him. Do you feel like you are precious to God?

EVERYONE DEPENDS ON GOD, HUMANS AND ANIMALS TOO

Job 12:7-10 NLT

"Just ask the animals, and they will teach you. Ask the birds of the sky, and they will tell you. Speak to the earth, and it will instruct you. Let the fish in the sea speak to you. For they all know that my disaster has come from the hand of the LORD. For the life of every living thing is in his hand, and the breath of every human being."

Alberto Opines

What in the world can I teach my Humans? I don't think they're interested in the skills I possess such as chasing mice or dismantling puzzles. And how does the earth instruct, or the fishes speak? I've never spoken to a fish. I'm an adventurous feline (the Male Human calls me "a dog in a cat suit", whatever that means). I've strolled in the garden and even waded in the downstairs pond. I have my own life vest for kayaking with the Female Human but I've yet to hear a fish speak or the earth instruct me about anything.

I pondered this verse from my perch on the wide window ledge. As I purrrused the woods below, it came to me. There is much to watch in those woods. I see the strong prey on the weak, and the fierce prey on the tame. If the Humans let me out, I'd be doing some preying myself. That's the way God designed things. It's all part of His plan. He doesn't punish the predator or the strong. He doesn't care for one animal more than another. He doesn't treat animals (or humans) according to their character.

God runs everything but He isn't a puppet master. We have free will. When the Female Human tells me not to dig my claws in the sofa, I have the freedom to obey or ignore her. I can choose to be a good kitty, and I am, sometimes.

God holds all of His creation in His hands. When humans care for their felines, they are reminded of their own reliance on the God of the Universe. Purrrsonally, I like knowing that God thinks animals have something to teach the humans. What have your animals taught you?

GOD'S PLAN FOR THE ANIMALS

Genesis 6:19 NLT

"Bring a pair of every kind of animal—a male and a female—into the boat with you to keep them alive during the flood."

Jasmine Opines

God took such trouble in creating all the animals of the earth. He charged Adam to name each one. When God decided to send the flood to this evil world, he made a covenant (a promise) with Noah and his family as well as the animals. When you humans bring animals into your home, you make a covenant with us, to care for us and to love us. Noah had a big job because God gave him the duty of caring for a representation of all creatures.

God can do anything. He could have flooded the earth and when He was finished and created new animals with a wave of His hand or the sound of His voice. Why didn't he do that? This kitty thinks it's because He was exhibiting His loving care for His creation. By saving a male and female from each type of animal, God showed us that what He created has value and that animals are not disposable. And just as He gave Noah the care of the animals on the ark, God gives our humans care of us. When our humans bring us into their lives for the duration of our lives, they are caring for us like Noah cared for the animals on the ark, just as God intended. Do you believe you have a covenant to care for the animals in your home?

MANS LAWS SHOULD NEVER ALLOW GOD'S CREATION TO BE PUT IN DANGER

Luke 14:5

"Then he turned to them and said, "Which of you doesn't work on the Sabbath? If your son or your cow falls into a pit don't you rush to get him out?"

Tucker Opines

In my many years, I've yet to see a cow or even a human fall into a pit. Actually, I'm not even sure what a cow looks like. And there's the fact that I have some "seeing" issues because of my crossed eyes. I have observed the Female Human rush outside to help a bird that smacked into our large windows, keeping it warm and finding a safe place for it until it revived enough to fly away again.

Our humans go to a place they call church (not to be confused with the place they go to called "work"). They tell me the day they go to the church place is called the Sabbath. This verse says you humans can work on the Sabbath if an emergency comes up. I know for a fact the Female Human extended first aid to some of those birds on the Sabbath. Evidently in old days you weren't supposed to do any work on the Sabbath, even if a poor hapless bird slammed into your window. Still, any discussion of work is immaterial to this Alpha feline. I never do any work, on the Sabbath or any other day.

If an animal or a human is in dire need of help, you shouldn't make an excuse that you can't offer assistance because of what day it is. Cat's never know, or care what day it is, nor do we need to. It seems to me that often you humans are more interested in following man's rules than God's rules. My fourteen years makes me wise which is why I'm in charge of The Tribe of

Five. I make the rules for our Tribe. Yet even the Tribe will acquiesce to human rules on occasion. When I hear, "Tucker, get off the kitchen counter", I may actually choose to obey the Female Human. If The Tribe of Five did everything they wanted and only followed their own rules, we might not have a home any more. We could get hurt. We understand that doing what those in charge of us want is ultimately good for us. This works the same for you humans. If you only do what you want, you may find yourself in trouble. God is in charge of all of us and obeying Him is a wise thing to do. Do you sometimes have a problem obeying God?

GOD IS THE CENTER OF HIS CREATED UNIVERSE

Psalm 104:24-25

"O LORD, what a variety of things you have made!   In wisdom you have made them all.   The earth is full of your creatures. Here is the ocean, vast and wide, teeming with life of every kind, both large and small."

Oliver Opines

We live in a house built into a hill. It has many windows. This provides me with an excellent view of the woods and all of God's creation around us. I love to lounge on the wide window ledges and look out at the cedar, aspen and pine trees, the little stream that runs along the ravine, the masked creatures that come to beg at the downstairs door and the elegant deer that come by to graze. I spend a great deal of time on those ledges. As I am a bit portly these days, I am I am thankful that the Humans had extra wide ledges designed for my comfort. As I look around I think how amazing it is that God created everything I see. And of course, God created me, this rotund little black and white feline! Still, as much as I see from my window perch, I haven't seen this ocean thing. Since it's vast and wide I'm guessing it's not the waterfall or the pond in the garden downstairs.

God did indeed create a variety of creatures and every morning when the female human fills the bird feeder, I see them, large and small. I wonder if all kitties get to see so much of God's creation. Do you humans appreciate God's creation as much as I do? Maybe you need to find a wide window ledge to stretch out on and enjoy the wonder of what God has made.

Anita Aurit

GOD OWNS EVERYTHING

Psalm 50:10-12

"For all the animals of the forest are mine, and I own the cattle on a thousand hills. I know every bird on the mountains, and all the animals of the field are mine. If I were hungry, I would not tell you, for all the world is mine and everything in it."

Alberto Opines

We have hills around our house but I can't count to a thousand. I'd guess we don't have a thousand hills though. I've never seen any cattle on those hills either. I suppose I have to trust that there are hills with cattle on them somewhere.

If God knows every bird on the mountain, does he know every kitty in the house? And if He does know every kitty, does that mean that when I jump on the counter and chew on the fruit basket (and sometimes the fruit) does God know that? If I sneak into a closet where I'm not supposed to be, does God know that? Meowza, purrhaps I need to think about being a better behaved kitty! I figured as long as the Humans didn't know what I was up to I was okay. Now I'm learning there is someone bigger, more important and all-seeing than our Humans and that's God! I wonder if all of you humans act as though you believe God sees everything you do.

The idea of God knowing my antics, and there are many, it is a bit unnerving. But God also says that the entire world is His. And He care for His world, even mischievous kitties.

I do wonder about the part where God says, "If I were hungry, I would not tell you." How will anyone know if God is hungry? And God is in control of everything so I'm not sure why or when He'd get hungry.

When I'm hungry I let my humans know, loudly. I am part Siamese after all. The Tribe needs our Humans, and our Humans need God. But God doesn't need His creation, nor does He depend on it like pets depend on you humans. Being part of God's creation means that are loved by God (and if we're lucky, humans too) and that we depend on Him. It's good to have someone to depend on. We depend on our humans. Do you humans depend on God?

GOD CARES ABOUT THE HEALTH AND WELL BEING OF HIS CREATION

Exodus 23:12a

"You have six days each week for your ordinary work, but on the seventh day you must stop working. This gives your ox and your donkey a chance to rest."

Lily Opines

First, allow me to remind you humans again that the concept of "work" is foreign to felines. I had to have the Female Human explain this "work" thing to me. She told me that when she and the Male Human leave the house five days per week, they go to this place called "work". Evidently this work is a very good thing for the Tribe as it allows them to buy our organic pet food and expensive cat toys and treats. She then explained that the two days they didn't go to the place called "work" was for them to rest and spend some time worshipping God. Poor humans! We felines rest all day and most of the night. If I were forced to go that place called "work" I don't think I'd make it! And evidently, there are animals that work. I don't know any personally and I'm very happy God didn't create me as one of those working animals. This feline was cut out to lounge on the sofa and permit her humans to give her head scratches. That's as much "work" as I'm interested in.

Once again God shows His love for His creation by telling humans to give their ox and donkey a rest. Evidently the ox and donkey are not as savvy as felines and allow humans to make them work. God wants the humans to rest and to give their animals a rest as well.

I'm glad that the humans take time to rest with us. It makes me happy to think that the animals that work for the humans get rest too. God is very thoughtful! Do you spend time and rest with those you love, two-legged and four-legged?

GOD INSTRUCTS HUMANS HOW TO CARE FOR HIS CREATION

Deuteronomy 22:6

"If you happen to find a bird's nest in a tree or on the ground, and there are young ones or eggs in it with the mother sitting in the nest, do not take the mother with the young."

Oliver Opines

God must have known that humans need some guidelines about caring for the animals He created. One would think you humans would know this. Sadly this is not true for all of you. Some folks even think cats should be vegetarians, meowzaa! In my own purrsonal experience, our Humans take wonderful care of us. I do know a bit about humans who don't care for cats. My brother Alberto and I came into the world as orphans as someone didn't care for our mother. She lived on the street and   was killed shortly after we were born. The good news is very soon after we lost our feline mother, we were rescued by a human mother. She fostered us until we were old enough to eat on our own and go to other foster homes.

This foster thing is very important to orphaned creatures. There are many amazing people who foster felines (and other animals). The Female Human even knows a lady who fosters orphaned deer until they can be released back into the woods. Whether it's a nest of little birds, motherless kittens or deer, God wants humans to leave animals with their mothers whenever possible. If there is no mother, He wants you humans to care for the orphaned creatures you come across.

Fostering is a noble and honorable thing for humans to do. If you've never tried it, I highly recommend it. One word of caution though, some folks have a hard time giving up the animals they foster, which is why the Tribe of Three became the Tribe of Five. Our Humans are foster failures and we're quite happy about that! Would you ever be willing to foster an animal for your local shelter?

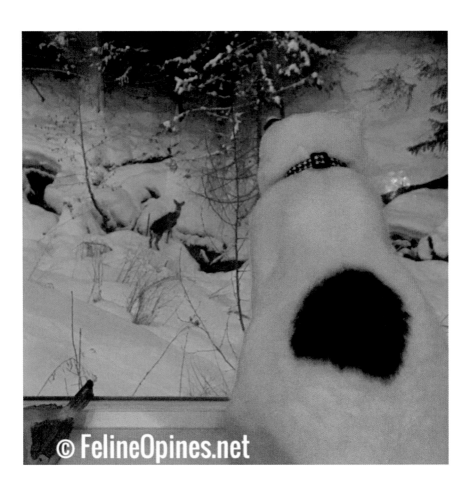

BE MINDFUL OF HOW THE ANIMALS IN YOUR CARE ARE DOING

Proverbs 27:23 NLT

"Know the state of your flocks, and put your heart into caring for your herds."

Tucker Opines

This wise feline believes the verse means humans should have more than one cat. And, if you substitute "Tribe" for the word "flock" I'd have to say God spoke to our Humans. The Male and Female Human definitely know the state of their Tribe. They are tuned in to how we react and how we're doing because they observe us closely. The Female Human is especially adept at reading our posture and facial expressions. She can always tell when we're not feeling well. There were several occasions when she whisked me off to the place with white coats just in time.

Seems to me that if humans are going to bring felines into their household, they'd want to pay attention to them, know their state and put their heart into caring for their pets. It makes me sad to know that some cats barely get a scratch behind the ear or playtime with their humans. If God is mindful of His creation, shouldn't you humans be mindful of us?

GOD PROVIDES FOR ALL, EVEN THE ANIMALS

2 Kings 3:17 NLT
"You will see neither wind nor rain, says the LORD, but this valley will be filled with water. You will have plenty for yourselves and your cattle and other animals".

Jasmine Opines

I've seen a lot of wind and rain from my throne on the window ledge. Thank goodness this prissy little feline doesn't have to be outside in it. What cat in her right mind wants to get her paws wet? And when there's no rain, God says He'll provide water for the people and the animals. Fetching my own water is not a task I ever have to worry about. I have Humans to provide that service.

I know God cares for the humans and provides for them so they in turn can provide for us (because it's all about us, or at least me, isn't it?). I may be a spoiled diva but I am thankful that animals are not an afterthought to God. He actually mentions us when He says "cattle and other animals". Of course He meant that cats were the "other animals". God is bigger than the view from my window or the land where we live. But this big God cares about all the animals including this little kitty and the rest of The Tribe of Five. If God cares for the cattle and the kitties, He cares for you too. And if you're worried about His provision, just be like a cat, rest happily and comfortably in the knowledge that He will provide all you need.

LET ALL PRAISE GOD!

Psalm 150:6 NLT
*"Let everything that breathes sing praises to the Lord!
Praise the Lord!"*

Final Thoughts, Alberto Opines

This opining about God brought The Tribe of Five to a consensus. All of God's creation should praise Him, indoor kitties and outside critters as well. Purrhaps The Tribe needs to have a conversation with our forests visitors in case they don't know about this. If the Tribe of Five has figured out this "praising" thing, you humans have figured it out too, right?

ABOUT THE AUTHOR

Anita Aurit lives in the Inland Northwest. She is a frequent speaker, and a published author in several genres. She is a professional member of CWA (Cat Writer's Association) and her blog FelineOpines.net is a muse medallion award winner. She has published a second "Feline Opines" book titled, "Felines Opine on Etiquette, What Humans Need to Know About Guests, Cat Sitters and Furniture". She is working on a cozy mystery entitled "Sit, Stay, Meow" which features Alberto and Oliver as primary characters. She is also working on the third "Felines Opine" book. You can learn more about Anita at AnitaAurit.com

Made in the USA
Columbia, SC
03 July 2023

20004329R00024